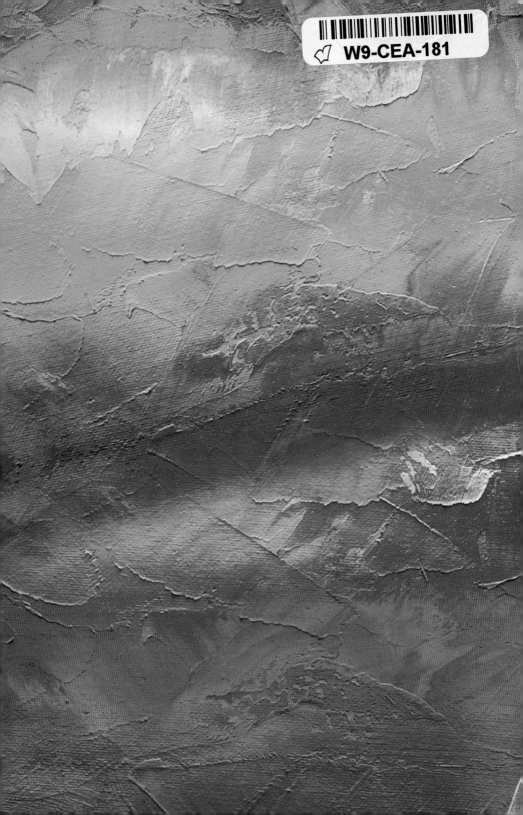

Leave. Me. Alone.

A Place to Drop Your Drama

Dylan Smith-Mitchell

Castle Point Books
New York

www.stmartins.com
www.castlepointbooks.com

The Castle Point Books trademark is owned by Castle Point Publishing, LLC.
Castle Point books are published and distributed by St. Martin's Press.

ISBN 978-1-250-20228-4 (trade paperback)

Cover design and illustration by Young Jin Lim
Interior design by Tara Long

Interior images used under license from Shutterstock.com

Our books may be purchased in bulk for promotional, educational, or
business use. Please contact your local bookseller or the Macmillan
Corporate and Premium Sales Department at 1-800-221-7945, extension
5442, or by email at MacmillanSpecialMarkets@macmillan.com.

First Edition: February 2019

10 9 8 7 6 5 4 3 2 1

THIS
JOURNAL
BELONGS
TO

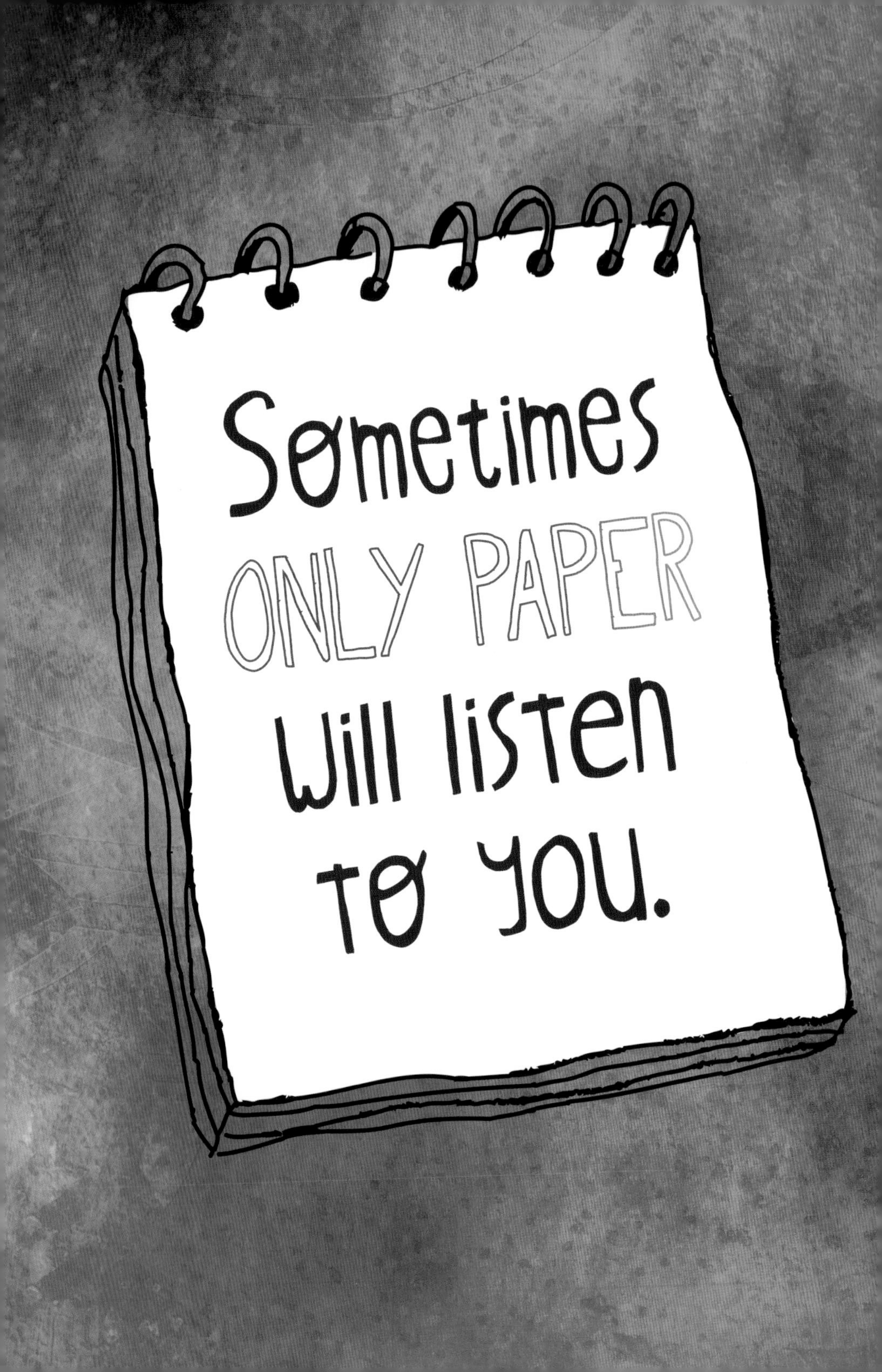
Sometimes
ONLY PAPER
will listen
to you.

Claim YOUR Space

EVER FEEL LIKE YOU'RE ALL ALONE? Your parents just give you *that look*, like you're not allowed to have a mood. Your friends? Well, they may think they can solve all the world's problems with *HMUs* on Snaps and stories. No one gets it. No one gets *you*. That's when it's okay to walk away and spend time with the person who knows you best.

Go find your space. Drop the filters. (No pressure to share anything with anyone!) And make your alone time just what you need. If you've got vents, dreams, secrets, goals, and a pen, this is the book to confide in. Here, there are no rules other than "You be you."

Start from the beginning with a page a day, or open to a page at random when you need it. Even when the rest of your life feels like it's spinning out of control, you're in control of your emotions and what you do with them.

BE MY Escape

If you could open the door to your room and enter another realm, where would you be? Someplace from history or what you imagine of the future? A setting from a book, video game, show, or movie? What makes you want to be here?

What comforts or thrills do you find in this place that you can bring into your real life?

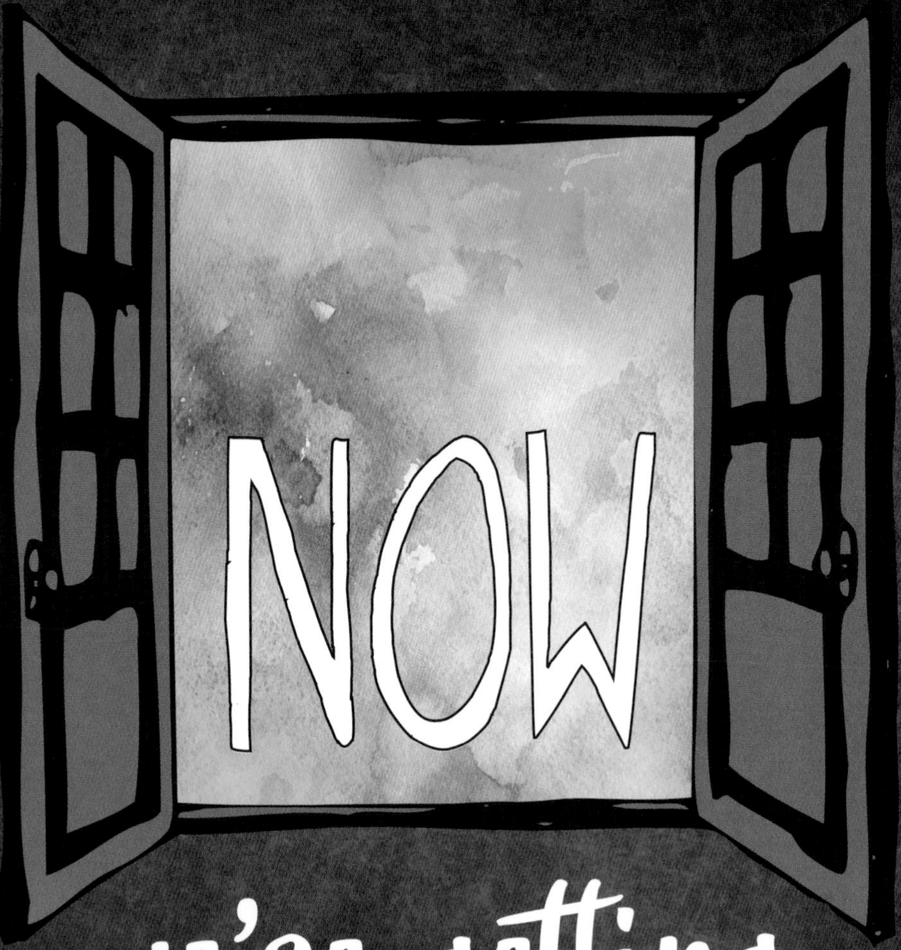

we're getting somewhere.

STOP Running

Who are you still chasing after that you need to release? An elementary school friend who's drifted away, a crush who doesn't return the feelings, a family member who made the choice to walk away a long time ago? Write that person a good-bye letter here, declaring your decision to move on.

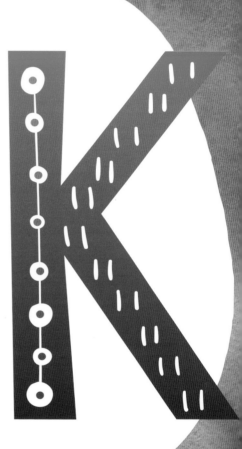

PRESSURE Valve

Sometimes it's okay to just be...okay. Not every experience or result is going to be GOAT. And in looking for a wow moment, sometimes we push aside all the little things that make the day pretty bearable. What went okay for you today? (Nothing is too insignificant!)

LOSE the Labels

Write your name on the label across from this page. Then cover this page with all the bad words and demeaning labels you've ever been called to your face, behind your back, on social media. Maybe there are some negative labels you give yourself when you're down.

Sure you've got them all? There's space on the back of this page as well. (Yep, go crazy!) Once you're feeling certain you've got them covered, tear out this page and choose your weapon of destruction—maybe the shredder, or just your bare hands! True story: You can't stop the name calling completely, but you can take away its power over you.

COME ON In

What people or places (physical, like a coffee shop, or virtual, like a gaming community) accept you—no matter what your mood? When have they seen you at your worst and not flinched?

Everyday ANCHORS

When everything else is chaos, what moments in your day can you rely on? They can be super-simple but still mean something to you. Maybe it's drinking from a favorite mug in the morning or barking back at that crazy dog down the street when you go by every day. Write or draw them here.

I will not get lost in a SEA OF DRAMA.

Playlist THERAPY

Music and moods are a perfect pairing. What songs help you
...get out a good cry?

...work out frustration?

...feel like you can handle anything?

...LOL?

It's time to
UNLOCK
& RESET.

Let It OUT

What did you want to say to someone so badly today? Maybe
you held back because the words would stir up trouble, or
maybe the right words only came to you when the moment was
past. Release them here and now.

GETTING Real

Putting on masks for others can be exhausting. What are you pretending to be that you're not? Why the act—and is it worth the energy to keep it up? If not, what's your exit scene?

CAPED Confessions

You are strong when you know your weaknesses. Wait, what?!
Think about it like this: once you have accepted your flaws,
no one can use them against you. List some of your biggest
struggles below. (Are you the queen of procrastination? A
no-filter mouth? A mess of moods?) How can you turn these
flaws into something to appreciate, or at least joke about?

Why So FAKE?

What teen characters from pop culture can you absolutely not stand? What bothers you about the way they rep the experience of being a teenager? Vent here.

Feelings Forecast

Emotions can be as unpredictable as the weather. How would you describe your state of mind in weather terms right now? If it's not so sunny, what's the last thing you remember that made you feel sunny?

Storms don't last forever.

Top FIVE

While possessions aren't everything, certain objects can give you feels. What five things in your room mean the most to you?

1. --

----

2. --

----

3. --

----

4. --

----

5. --

Mine, Mine!

Feel like there's a constant tug on your time and emotions?
Imagine you have an entire day to spend any way you'd like.
What's your pleasure?

How can you make even just a part (or feeling) of that day
come true soon?

Stir IT UP

Stormy Skies. Jungle Green. Diva Purple. Peaceful Seas. Imagine a paint color is named after your vibe. What does the color look like, and what's its killer name? What mood do you want it to bring to those who use it?

Color

my

many

moods.

READY Player

If your life were made into a video game, what would the obstacles look like? What would be the goal? What gets bonus points in your virtual world?

Casting Call

If you were to create the ultimate YouTube channel, what topics and perspectives would you cover, and who would your experts include? What would you call your channel?

My teachers step outside the classroom.

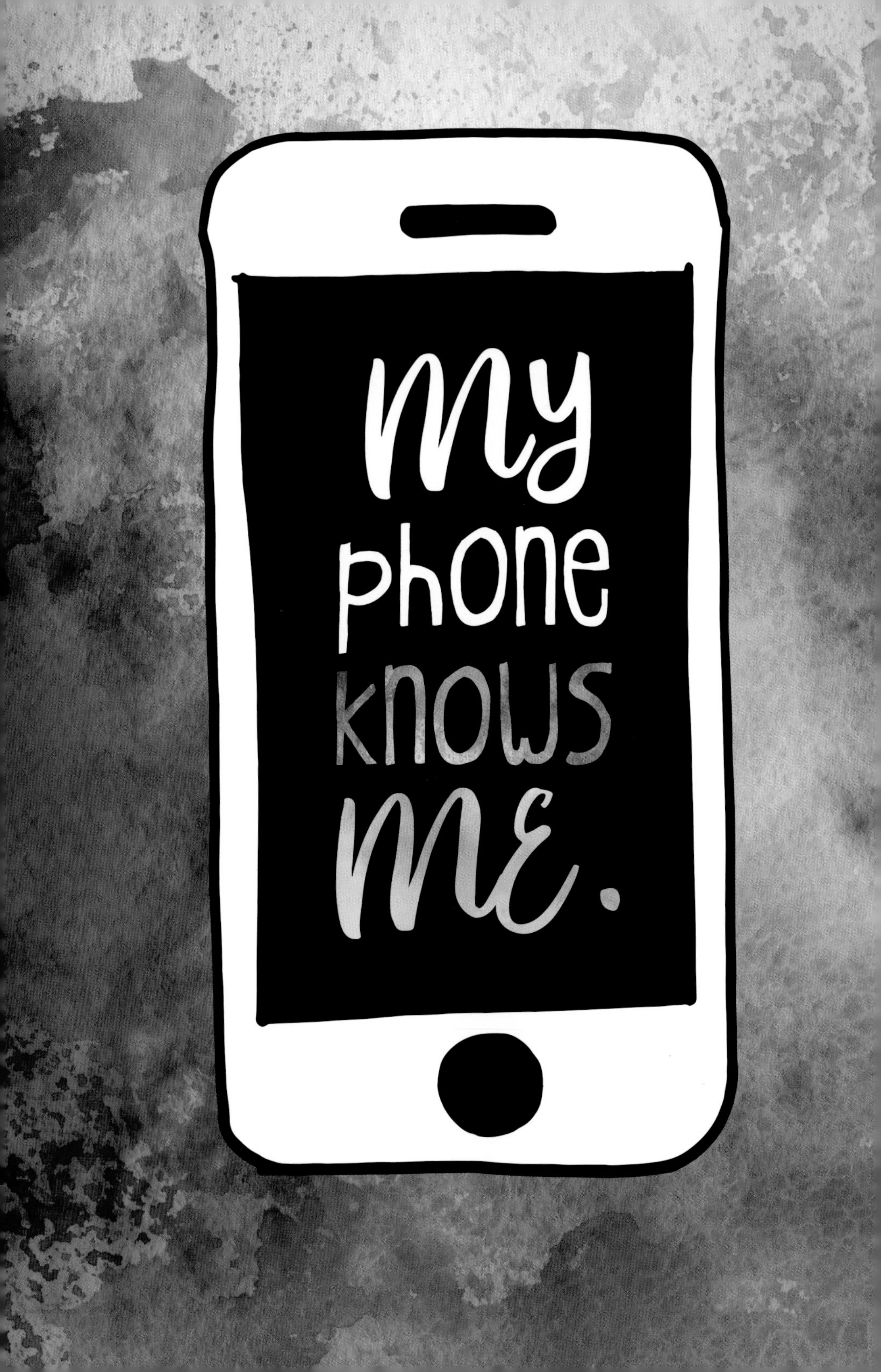
my
phone
knows
me.

Hear THIS!

What are the current ringtones or alerts for your top contacts?
What do the songs or sounds mean to you?

Ctrl Z

Can I get a
DO-OVER?

Real Regrets

What recent event in your life do you most wish you could apply autocorrect to?

_____

_____

_____

_____

_____

Even if you can't take things back completely, is there anything you can do to improve the current situation?

_____

_____

_____

_____

Hello?!

"I love you." "I hate you." "We need to talk." Who needs a billboard to get the message—and what is the all-important message you're sending?

GO There

Think of a time you felt like everything was right in the world. Where were you and what were you doing?

Can you find a way to recreate that feeling when you need a boost?

No Invaders

You now rule your own private island. If anyone wants to come and live here, what are the top rules they need to follow?

NAME THE Hurricanes

Hurricanes are inevitable in nature and in our lives. Who are the hurricanes in your life, and what's their damage level?

What's your recovery plan when they strike, and who can help?

Solve my mystery.

It's Our *Secret*

What's one thing no one knows about you? Why haven't you shared it with anyone? Will you ever allow a big reveal beyond these pages?

Can I get the
ANSWER KEY?

Absolutely No Clue

Big or small, what one question have you always wanted answered? Is there a way to get the answer—or at least edge a little closer?

TOY Story

What toy or activity from your childhood do you miss? What feeling did it give you? Make a plan to rediscover it while no one's watching.

We're all a little afraid of the dark.

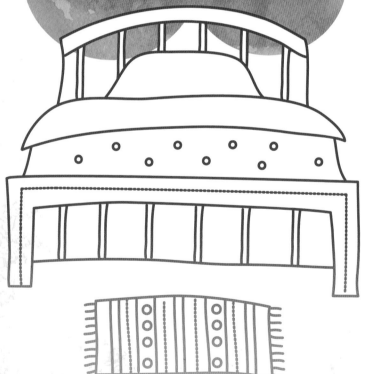

My Monsters

There are probably a lot of nightmares and fears you've outgrown. But what still makes you want to hide under the bed?

What makes you feel safe?

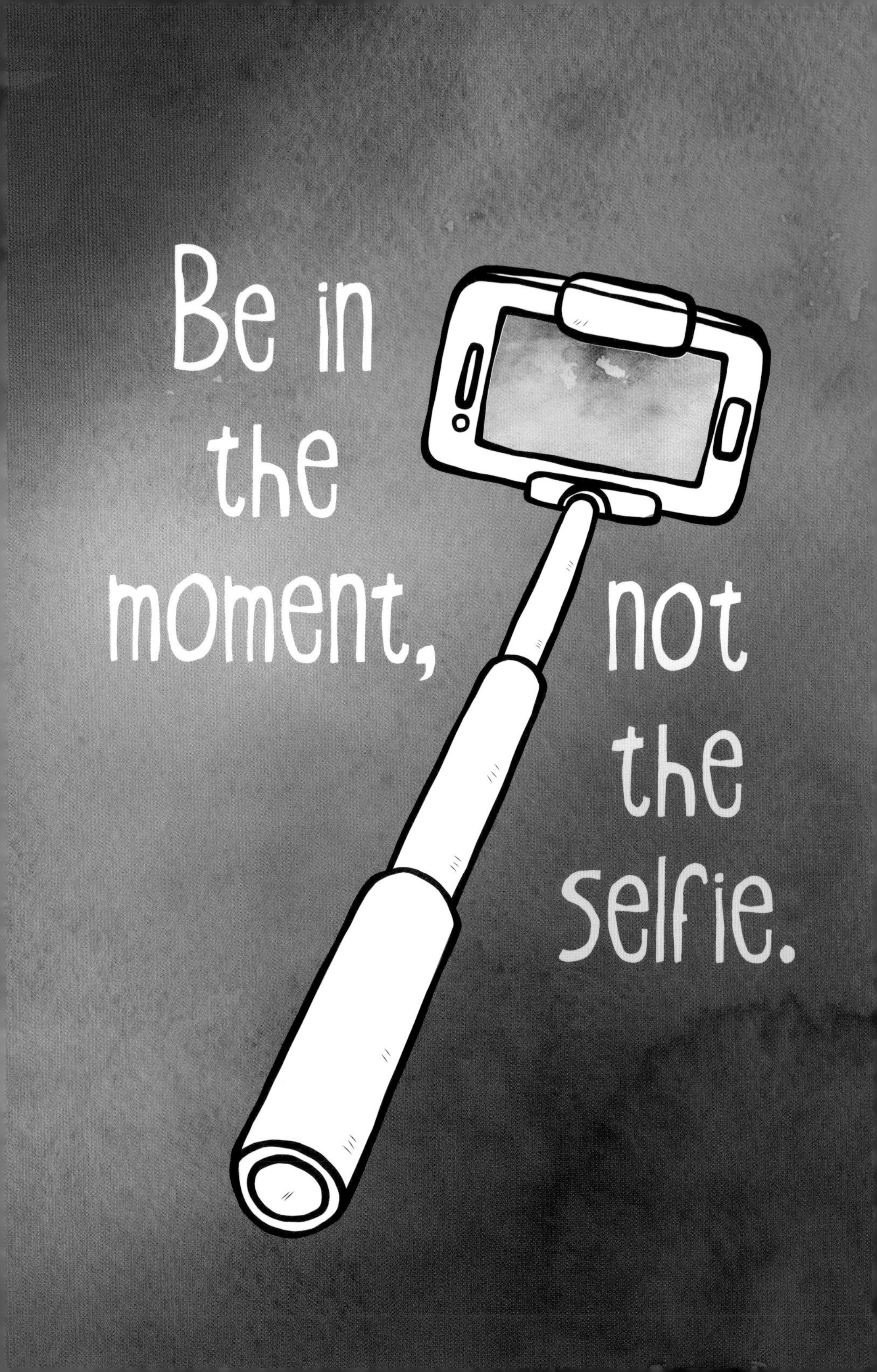
Be in the moment, not the selfie.

True Portraits

Find a photo in which you're smiling or laughing (not posed!).
Attach it below, and recall what you were doing and any
partners in crime. Make a plan to do that thing or connect with
that crowd this week.

Hacking the Halls

If you could wave a magic wand and change five things about your school, what would they be?

1. _____

_____

2. _____

_____

3. _____

_____

4. _____

_____

5. _____

_____

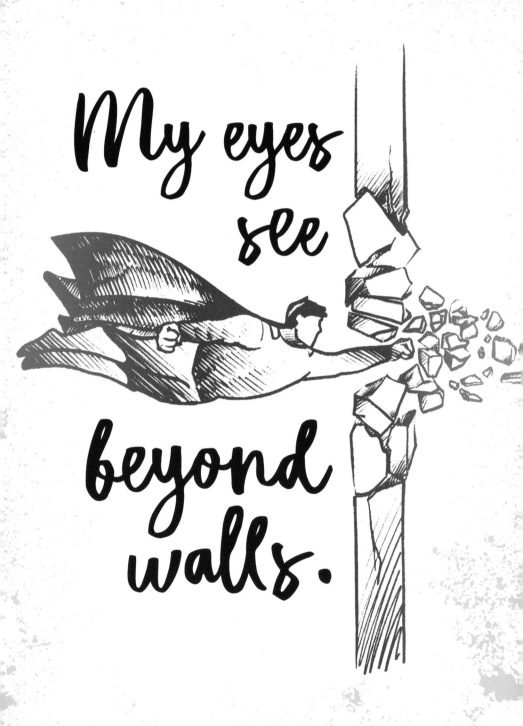

Do YOU See It?

What's the view out your bedroom window?

What do you wish the view were?

Rep Reveal

We love to say we don't care what others think. But it's only natural to wonder about others' impressions of you. What do you want people to say about you when you're not around?

Are there healthy changes you can make to boost the positive vibes you give off?

Give me
VITAMIN D
skies.

Outdoor Recess

When you just need to get away, where can you go outdoors to breathe in freedom and breathe out the nonsense?

_____

_____

_____

_____

_____

_____

_____

_____

_____

_____

It's an interesting story...

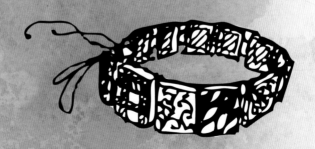

WHAT'S YOUR Mark?

Imagine that you need to introduce yourself and illustrate all that is important to you through a tattoo or a charm on a necklace or bracelet. Draw what it would look like.

Worlds COLLIDE

If your online, social personality came off the screen into real life, in what ways would you be clones? In what ways would you not even recognize each other?

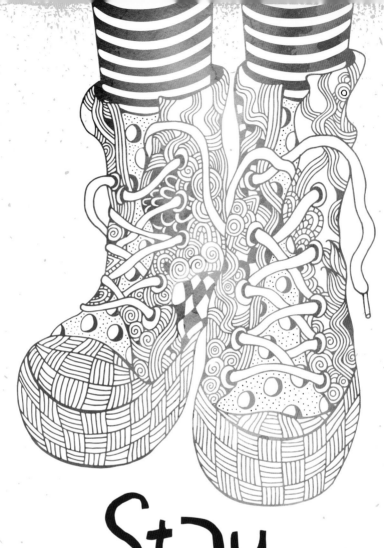

Stay
weird.

Celebrate the Crazy

Isn't a little ridiculous better than boring? List 10 things about yourself that are weird but wonderful.

1. ---

2. ---

3. ---

4. ---

5. ---

6. ---

7. ---

8. ---

9. ---

10. --

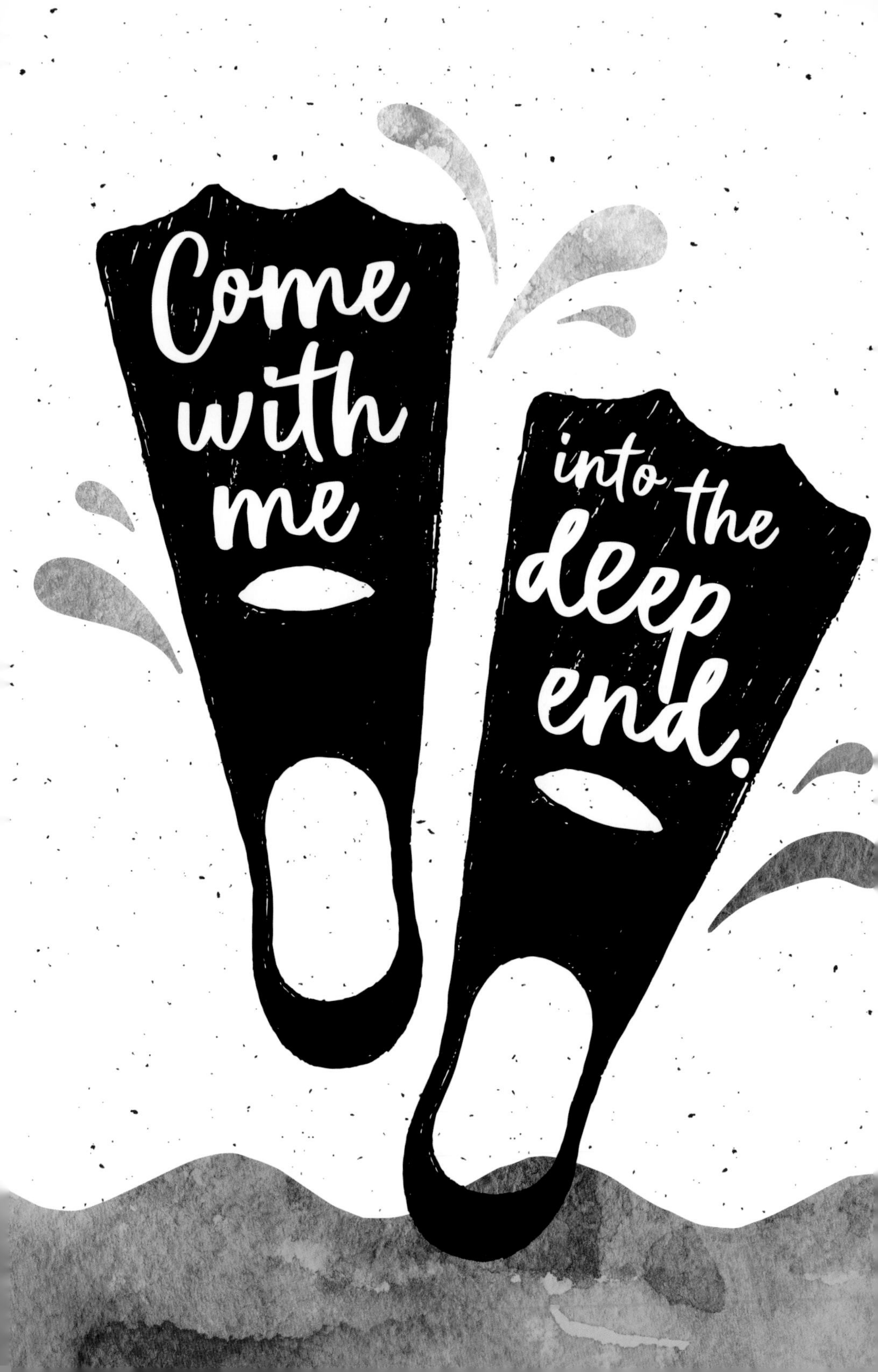
Come with me
into the deep end.

Out of the Shallow

Sometimes we keep our depths hidden. What do people not see when they first meet you that you wish they would discover sooner?

All Kinds OF GOALS

Why so serious? Not all goals need to center on school or sports. What goals are important to you in the next year? Make sure you include some just for fun and for bringing out the best you.

WATCH MORE *sunsets* THAN *Netflix.*

Take in the beauty;

leave the baggage.

Hometown Flavor

Places come with their own peculiar pros and cons. How does where you live make your life better? What can you discover and do right where you are?

How does where you live make days more challenging? What limitations do you face, and how can you get past them?

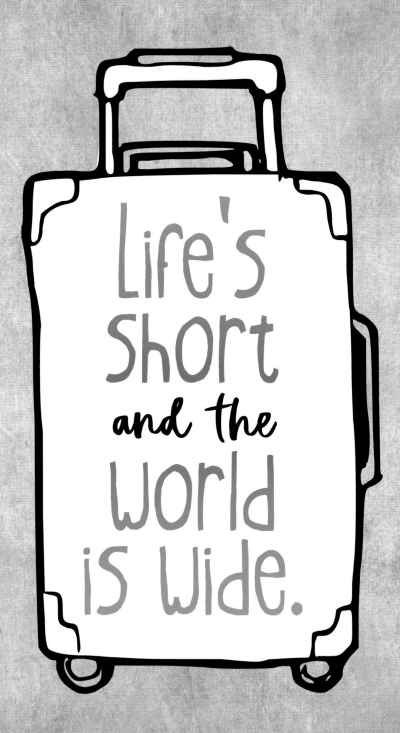

Adventures Ahead

What destinations do you dream of traveling to in the future?
Where do your adventures begin, and when?

What do you need to do or know before you go?

Speak to Me

Whether they come from an author, a celebrity, your best friend, or even a parent (it won't go beyond these pages!), what words of wisdom, inspiration, or venting hold special meaning for you? At what moments in your life have they helped you?

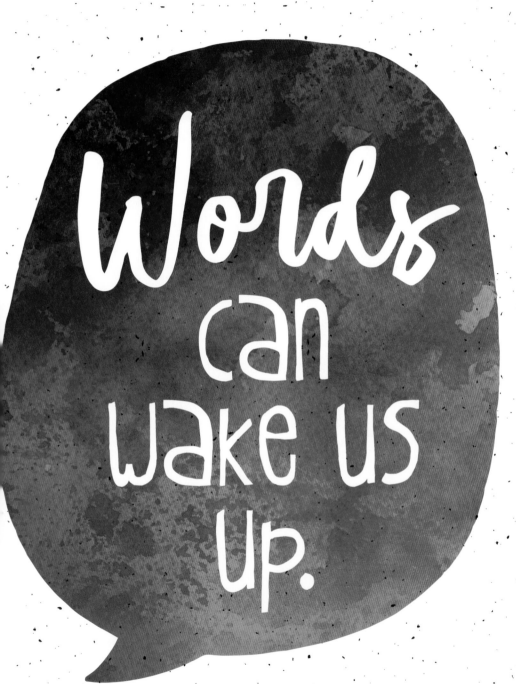

Love your decisions, not others' opinions of them.

Sounds About Right

We make tons of choices every day—and some turn out better than others, to say the least. What's the best choice you've ever made?

How did you know it was the right choice at the time?

Permission to Release

Holding in emotions and keeping it all together 24/7 can be a setup for a major crash. It's healthy to allow some release before it comes to a bigger break. When was the last time you cried?

_____

_____

_____

_____

_____

How did you feel afterward?

_____

_____

_____

_____

_____

Just Between Us

From secret nicknames to displays of affection, what odd ways do you show you care with your friends, family, crush?

People you can be crazy with

= EVERYTHING.

BE
BETTER
than BASIC.

Do Hard Things

There are always going to be two paths in life: the easy one and the hard one. And they usually lead to very different places and degrees of rewards. What hard thing have you done that you once thought you never could, and how did it feel to take that path?

What's the next challenge you need to conquer?

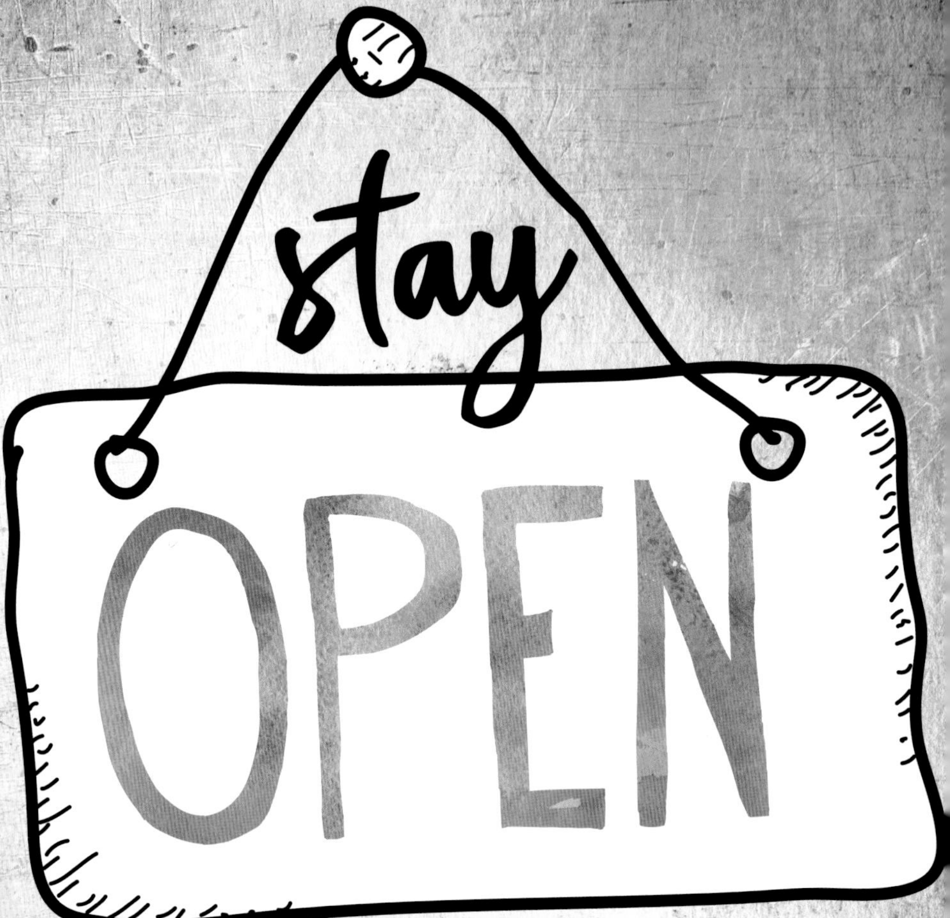

to what wanders in.

Sorry for the Slam!

There's a saying (or maybe it's a fortune cookie?) that goes, "Happiness often sneaks in a door you didn't think was open." Are there people or experiences in your life that you slammed the door on too quickly? How can you let them know that the door is inching open again?

STORY Support

When you write the story of your life, whose name(s) do you want to appear in it a billion times? What has earned them that position?

You
are the
characters
in my life.

I DECIDE THE VIBE.

APPS *with Attitude*

What apps put you in a better mood instantly? And which ones just seem to feed your low feelings?

What plan can you make to use the apps that lift your emotions more than the ones that bring you down?

My View

What do you see so differently than everyone around you?
Does it bother you that no one else relates?

Why do you think you have a different idea?

Whatever sprinkles your doughnuts.

Smiles and Smiles

Cover this page with random (big and little!) things that make you happy.

Face IT

What have you been you putting off—a decision, a conversation, an apology? Decide now when and where you will stop the flight and move forward.

Exhale the extra.

Take a PASS

What has everyone been making a huge deal over lately that clearly doesn't deserve your time and attention?

How can you walk away without adding to the drama?

Keep Climbing

What great things are you looking forward to...in the next
few months?

...in the next few years?

Be My "Cheese"

Who can you count on to always make you smile? Remember five times this person came to your rescue and pulled you up.

1. --

----

2. --

----

3. --

----

4. --

----

5. --

I'M
WEARING
the smile
YOU 😄
GAVE ME.

Before and After

Maybe it was meeting someone new. It could have been a text or call that cleared up a misunderstanding. Or did you finally reach a goal you set for yourself? What moments from the past year changed everything for you?

TIME TO *Reverse*

Are there situations you've gotten pulled into that aren't yours to own? How can you back out and let the true parties involved take it from here?

Me and Free

When do you like to be alone? How much alone time do you need each week?

Little Bit Lazy

Some retreat from the craziness is okay. What's your favorite way to be lazy, and how do you limit the time so it doesn't put your life on hold too long?

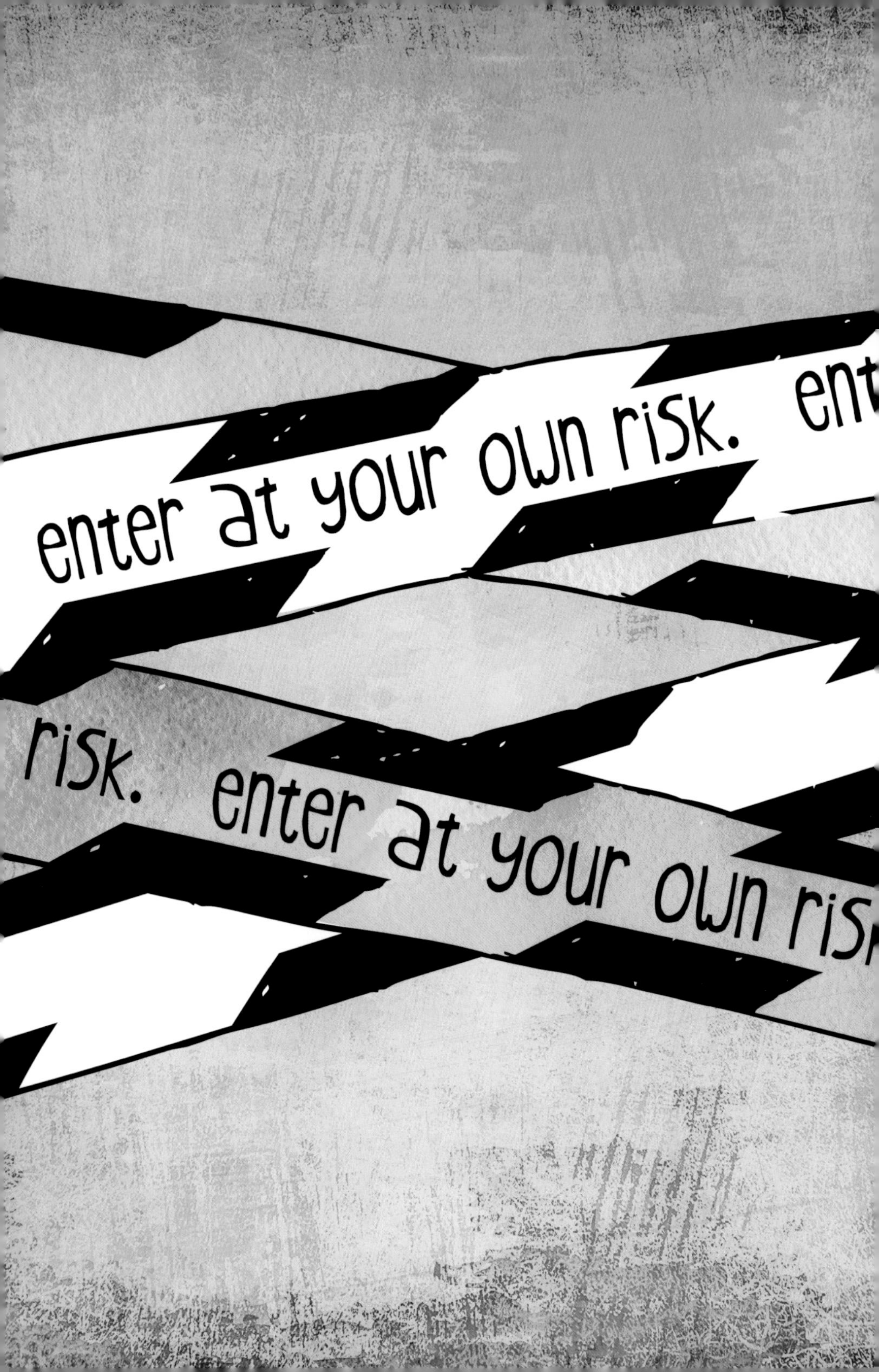
enter at your own risk. ent
risk. enter at your own ris

Construction Zone

What part of your life feels like it's constantly under construction—maybe even demolition?

What acts as your safety helmet as you go through the mess?

savage or sweetheart?

Or Something In Between?

Would your friends characterize you as more savage or more sweetheart, and why? Is the answer the same for your family?

Are you okay with this assessment, or would you like to add a little more savage or a little more sweet?

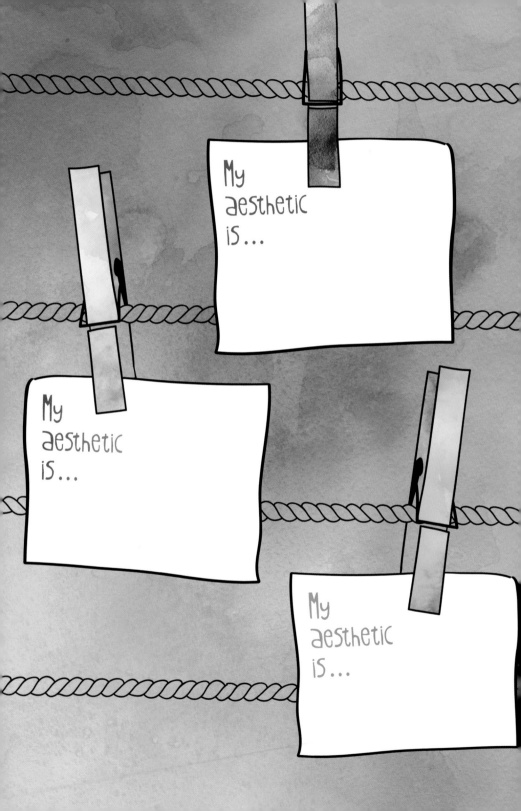

Sum It Up

What answer(s) to the fill-in-the-blank on the previous page match your mood today? Jot them down or add images below.

No More Delays

What have you always wanted to do that you keep putting off? How can you make that adventure or wish come to life this year?

Send it!

this month

Give Them a Surprise!

Who is underestimating you in your life right now? How will you prove them wrong?

Love Fool

Opening up to a mad rush of feelings is seriously scary. What risks have you taken for love?

Are there risks you regret *not* taking? (Is it truly too late?)

Never STOP FIGHTING

We often get into the biggest emotional conflicts with the people we care most about. If we didn't care, we wouldn't put up a fuss. What's the worst fight you've ever had with a friend or family member?

How did the relationship get repaired, or are you still working on it?

You're worth fighting for.

Until I saw this, I didn't know what beautiful meant.

Through My Eyes

What do you consider beautiful? Use words, photos, and drawings to capture beauty below.

Not luck.
I deserved it.

The Payoff

What is something you worked super-hard for and poured your
soul into, and it paid off? How did the effort feel? How did the
result feel?

Head vs. Heart

Which do you tend to follow—and do the results turn out okay?

Is there a way to find a balance between your head and your heart?

HEAD UP,

HEART STRONG.

What's trending?
You being you.

Your Own Course

Hashtag today, gone tomorrow. What trend are you proud of yourself for not following?

Is there a positive trend you've started or could start?

We're all
JUST KIDS
who left the
playground.

When I Grow Up

What did you think it would be like to be a teenager when you were younger? What parts turned out to be true, and where were you way off in your expectations?

What would you tell younger kids about becoming a teenager?

No Returns Allowed

We often spend too much time imagining parts of ourselves we'd love to change. What parts of yourself would you never want to trade in?

NEVER STOP
making memories.

YOU Back Again?

If you could return to any day of your life so far and relive it just one more time from start to finish, which day would you choose, and why?

They're not perfect,

but they're mine.

Fam Life

If you could change three things about your family, what would they be?

1. --

----

2. --

----

3. --

What would you never want to change about your family?

Go Away!

If you could invent a new kind of spray repellent (beyond insects!), who or what annoyances would you design it to keep away?

MY SECRET
TALENT IS
slaying.

Check It Out

Whether serious, like playing the uke, or crazy, like drawing with your toes, what hidden talents do you have that no one knows about (or at least, not most people)?

What talents do you wish you had? Can you go forward with any of these?

If you're going to fail,

make it epic.

NO Worries

You've probably heard adults say to you, "You can't have everything." What are three things you're terrible at—but you totally don't care?

1. _____

_____

_____

2. _____

_____

_____

3. _____

_____

_____

Ten Reasons Why

What words would your best friends and family use to describe you and why they like spending time with you?

1. --

2. --

3. --

4. --

5. --

6. --

7. --

8. --

9. --

10. ---

Friendship
isn't a big thing.
It's millions of small things.

Exit PLAN

There's only so much pressure you can take. What isn't worth your mental energy right now? Consider your activities, relationships, doubts, and fears. Write below what you need to release, then rip out the page and send it flying as a paper airplane or crumple it into a ball targeted for the trash—whichever style is right for you.